Ivano Vincenzo Granata

*4 compositions
on the theme of cold*

for soprano saxophone

Symbols

Flatterzunge: produced by rolling the tongue against the palate, taking the mouthpiece at the tip will let the reed and the tongue free to flutter without any obstruction.

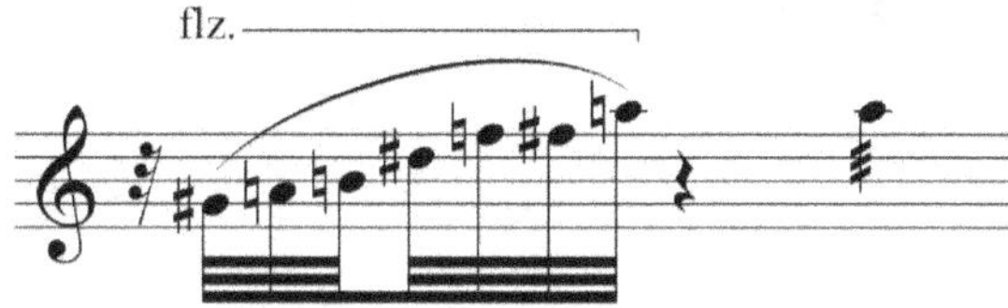

Glissando: can be produced either with the lips and oral cavity or by gradual movement of the keys.

Key noise: consists in a percussive effect obtained by slapping down the pads without blowing, keeping the mouthpiece in the mouth to obtain the given pitch.

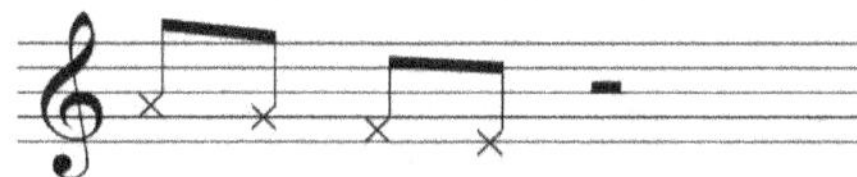

Slap tongue: it is produced by pressing the reed against the mouthpiece, thus creating a vacuum before the tongue is quickly withdrawn.

Multiphonics: simultaneous production of more than one audible tone, produced by using specific fingering.

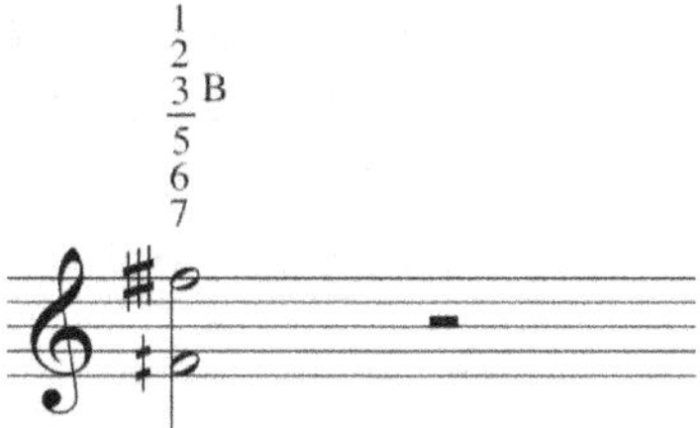

Breath noise: audible breath sound, can mix or replace the given tone.

Overtone: while fingering the lower pitch, use the oral muscles to perform the higher pitch.

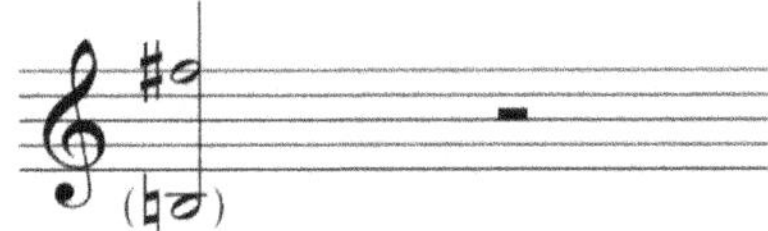

Bisbigliando: microtonal trills, obtained by shifting the embouchure or throat muscles, or using specialised fingerings (playing a tone while repeatedly lowering, or raising, a non-essential key).

Growl: consists of singing randomly when playing loud.

Bend: While blowing a note move the tongue away from the reed back towards the throat, without changing its shape, it should be open, letting the air pass as usual.

Subtone: It consists in a lower-jaw pressure that is replaced by the tongue under the lip, or the tongue lightly touching the reed (as if pronouncing the word "the"). Alternatively, the embouchure can be moved towards the end of the mouthpiece, holding it only with the lips and without pressure from the teeth (in each case the reed is partially prevented from vibrating and the upper partials are subdued).

Frozen

Névé

Iceberg

Shelter

duration: c. 11 minutes

Frozen

(giacciato)

Frozen

Ivano Vincenzo Granata

Frozen

Frozen
f
p
mp
f
mp
mf
mp
mf
mp
5
fp
fff
p
2 3 4 5 6 Bb
2 3 4 5 6 C1 Bb
1 2 3 5 7 Bb C5 C6
p
6
p
3
3
3
3
non vibr.
vibr. ord.
accel.
a tempo
growl
f

Frozen
mp
f
p
mp
1
2 C1
3 (B♭)
4
5
7
1
2
3 B♭
5
6
7
6
subtone
53
mp
6
3
3
3
normal
molto vibr.
accel.
poco vibr.
vibr. ord.
56
p
f
ppp
p
mp
a tempo
60
62
f
f
0

Névé

(firn)

Névé

Ivano Vincenzo Granata
♩ = 60 misterioso
gliss.
gradually changing
rit.

Iceberg

(iceberg)

Iceberg

Iceberg
growl
normal
normal
growl
normal

Iceberg

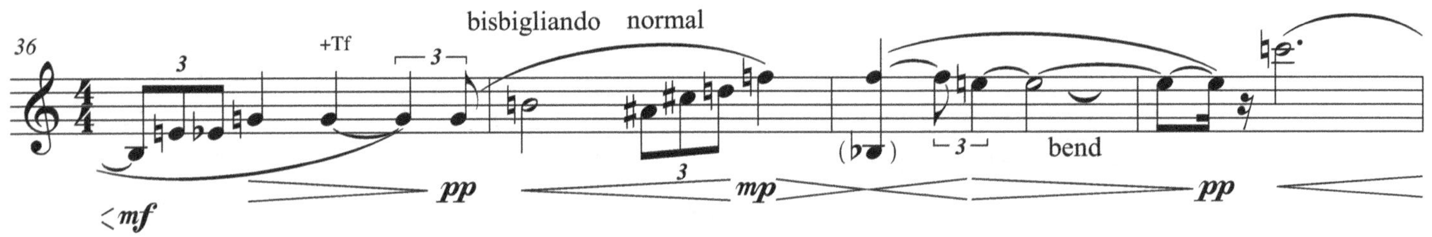

Iceberg

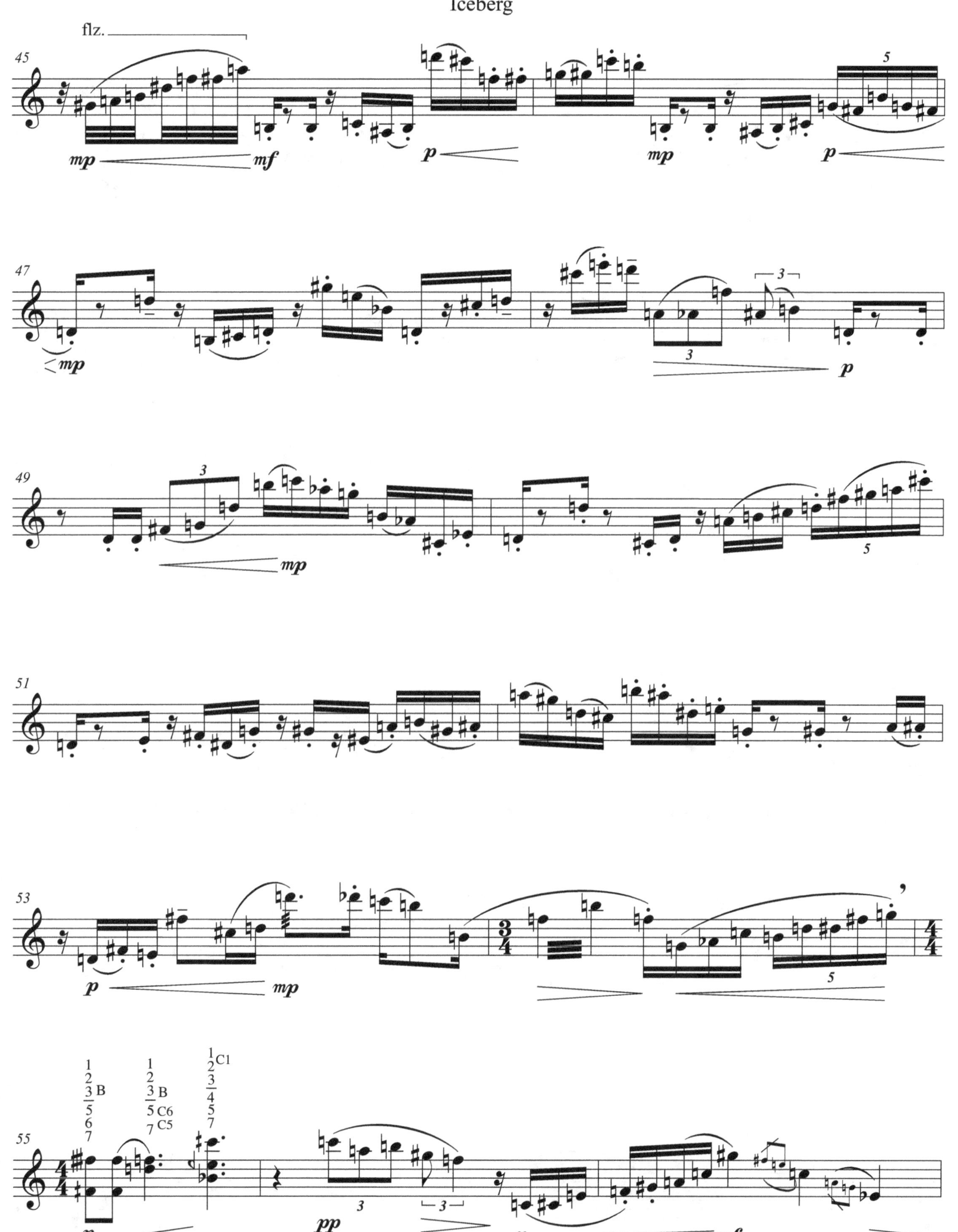

Iceberg

Shelter

(rifugio)

Shelter

Ivano Vincenzo Granata

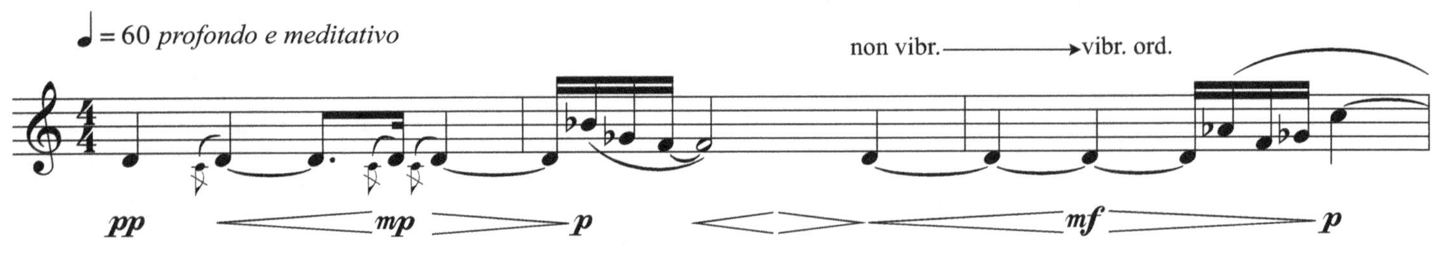

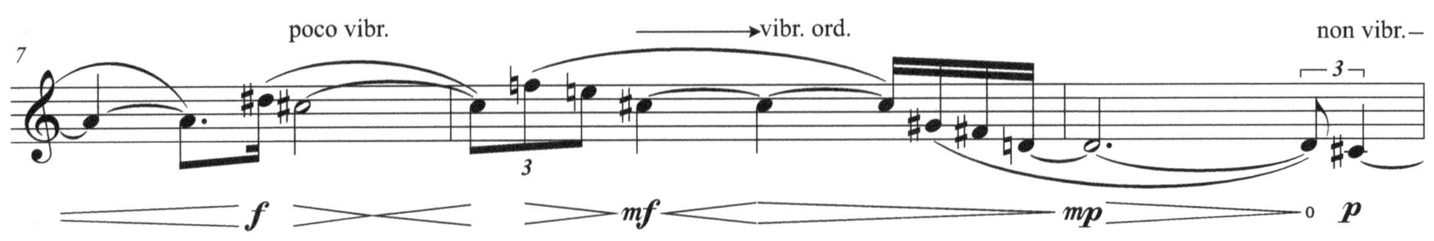

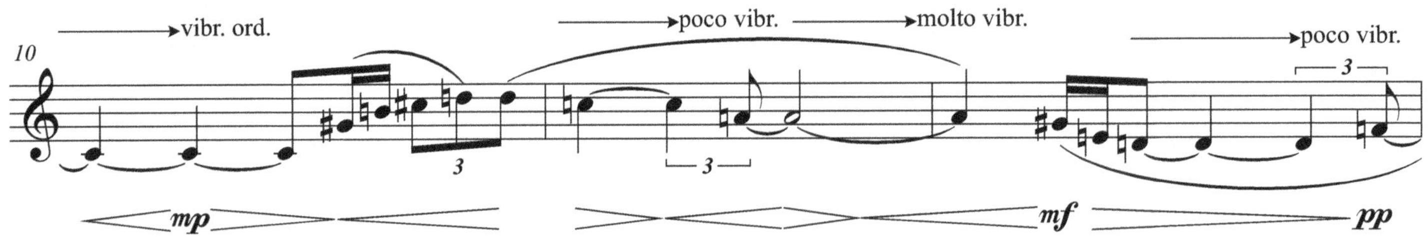

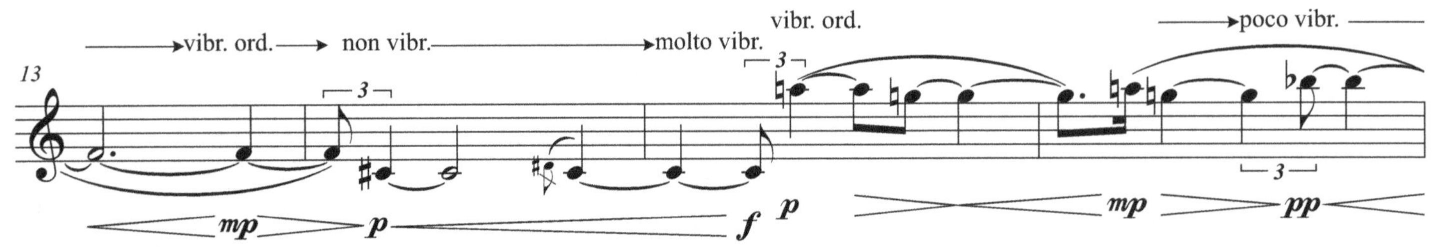

Shelter

Italy, September 2022
www.ivan-granata.com

www.ingramcontent.com/pod-product-compliance
Lightning Source LLC
Chambersburg PA
CBHW080732120726
48001CB00010B/3207